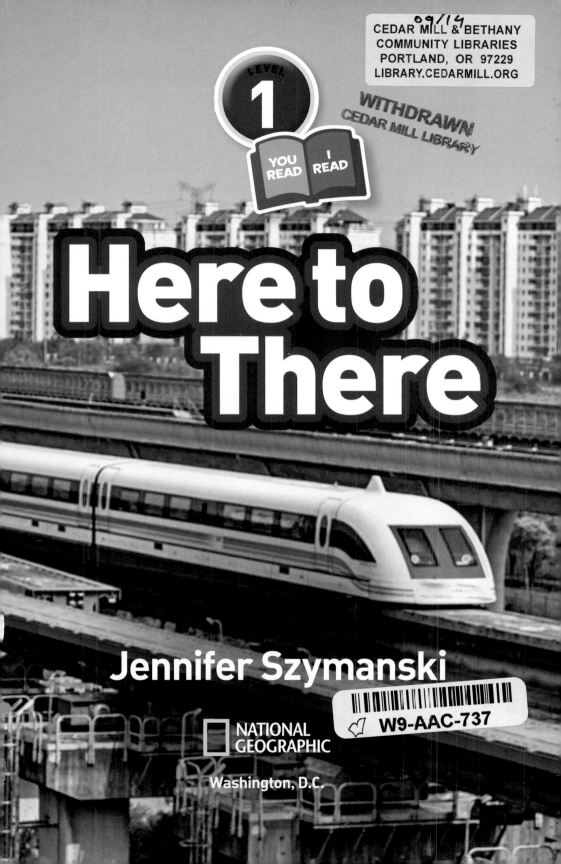

LEVEL
1
YOU READ · I READ

Here to There

Jennifer Szymanski

NATIONAL GEOGRAPHIC

Washington, D.C.

How to Use This Book

Reading together is fun! When older and younger readers share the experience, it opens the door to new learning. As you read together, talk about what you learn.

YOU READ

This side is for a parent, older sibling, or older friend. Before reading each page, take a look at the words and pictures. Talk about what you see. Point out words that might be hard for the younger reader.

I READ

This side is for the younger reader.

As you read, look for the bolded words. Talk about them before you read. In each chapter, the bolded words are: Chapter 1: travel verbs • Chapter 2: adverbs and prepositions • Chapter 3: parts of vehicles • Chapter 4: describing words

At the end of each chapter, do the activity together.

YOUR TURN!

Make a paper airplane! Follow the directions. Use the pictures to help you.

Table of Contents

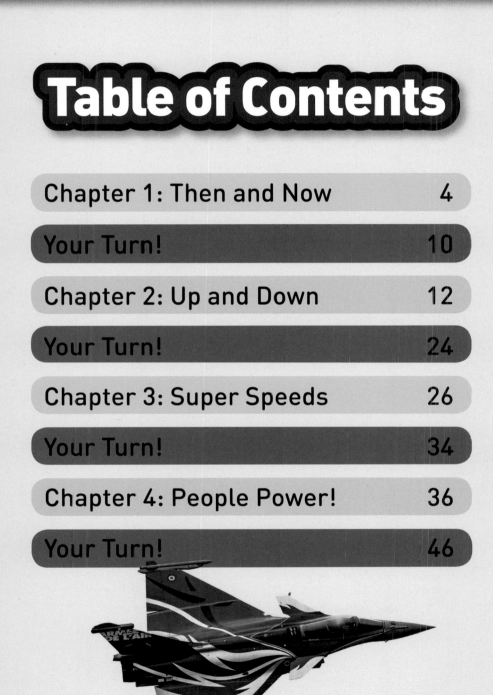

CHAPTER 1

Then and Now

Look around! It seems like people are always on the move. They **go** to work or school, and take trips for fun. They also explore new places.

Boats **go** on water.
Cars and trains go on land.
Planes go in the sky.

YOU READ People have always had ways to travel. Long ago, wind, animals, or people made things **move**. Wind pushed boats. Animals pulled carts.

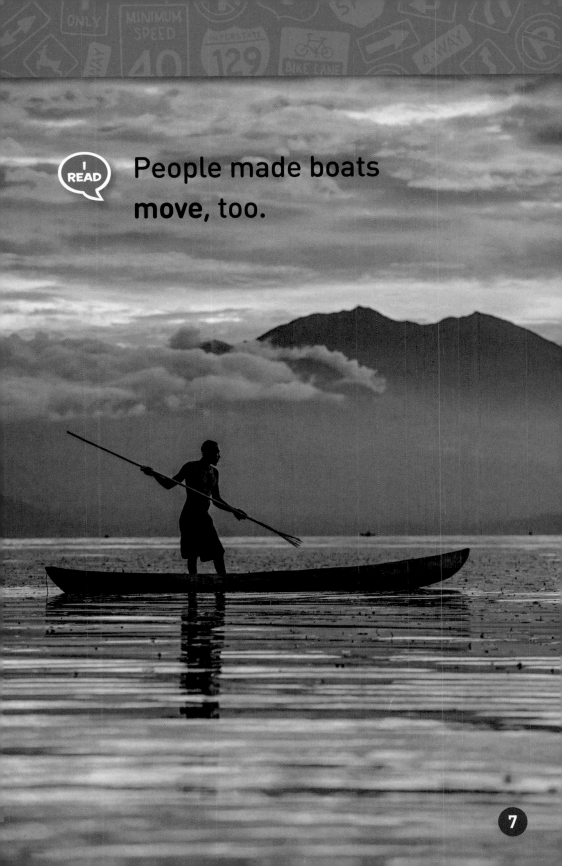

READ People made boats **move**, too.

YOU READ

Today, we have many ways to **travel**! Wind, animals, and people can still make things move. But cars, trains, planes, and boats can go fast. They get power from fuel, electricity, or the sun.

This car can **travel** without a driver! It knows when to stop and when to go.

YOUR TURN!

How do you get around your neighborhood? Think of a place near your home or school. Describe how you would get to that place. Would you walk, bike, take a bus or subway, or ride in a car?

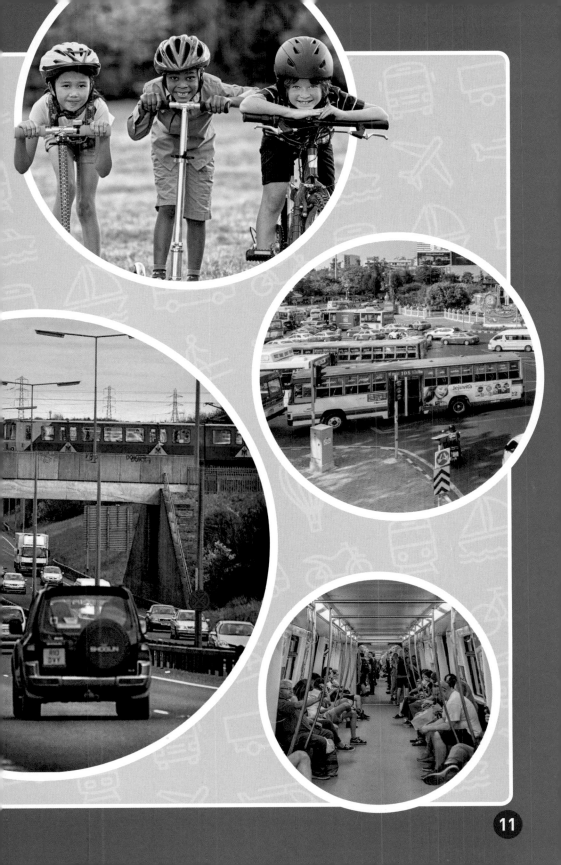

CHAPTER 2

Up and Down

YOU READ Some things go up and down. Hang gliders do that! They soar **above** the Earth.

The glider is like a big kite. The rider flies high **above** the trees.

YOU READ

An airship floats above a city. Passengers watch the scenery **beneath** them as the ship moves through the air.

I READ People stand in baskets **beneath** these hot-air balloons. Soon, they float into the sky.

This cable car uses a strong wire to go up and down. The wire is called a cable. The car's wheels roll **along** the cable to take people up a mountain.

These cars move up and down a big hill. A cable pulls them **along** a track.

Some planes are so big that they have two floors! There is lots of room **inside** this plane for people and cargo.

There is not much room in this plane. Only the pilot can fit **inside**.

YOU READ

Submarines take people deep **below** the surface of the ocean. People in this submarine learn about animals that live on the ocean floor.

 People ride the subway. The train goes **below** the city.

 Helicopters are smaller and lighter than most airplanes. They can fly straight up and down, and they can take off **from** and land almost anywhere.

Seaplanes can take off **from** water. They can land there, too.

YOUR TURN!

Make a paper airplane!
Follow the directions. Use
the pictures to help you.

Fold a piece of paper in half the long way. Open it back up. You should see a crease running up and down the paper.

1

2

Fold one of the top corners in to the crease in the middle. Fold in the other corner the same way. When you are done, you should have something that looks like a triangle at the top.

Fold one of the sides of the triangle in to the middle crease. Do the same thing with the other triangle's side. When you are done, it should look like two larger triangles pointing up at the top.

3

Fold the whole paper in half the long way on the middle crease. The triangles should be inside.

4

Hold the paper so the point is pointing to the right. Fold down the top flap so the top edge meets the bottom edge to make a wing. Turn the paper over. Do the same thing to make the other wing.

5

6

Hold your plane by the bottom. Throw it gently into the air and let it fly!

CHAPTER 3
Super Speeds

YOU READ Jet planes can fly very high in the sky. Their **engines** help them fly faster than other kinds of planes.

This car has the same **engines** as some jets. It is the fastest car in the world!

YOU READ

You can see right under this ferry! Only the bottom edges of its **hull** touch the water. That helps the boat move fast.

There's air between the **hull** of this boat and the water. That makes the boat glide on the water. It moves fast!

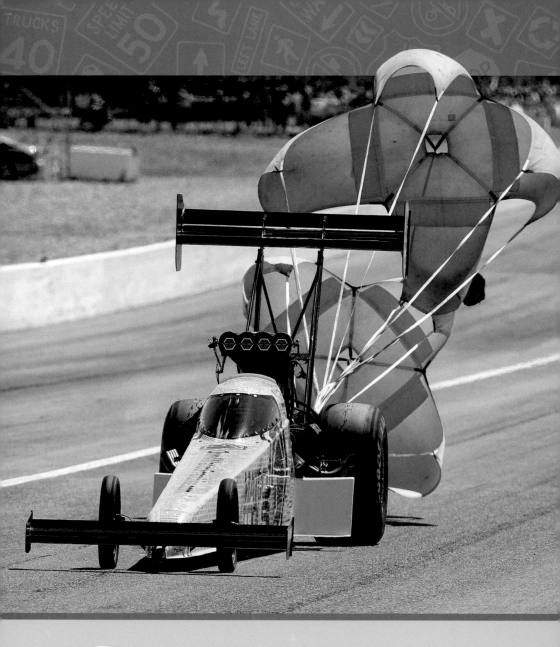

When you go fast, you need to be safe! Some cars need help slowing down after going so fast. It takes a parachute and brakes to stop this drag racer's **wheels**.

These cars have wide **wheels**. That helps them go around turns.

YOU READ

If you're in a hurry, you could take this train! There are magnets attached to the underside of this train. There are also magnets in the **rails** below the train. The magnets push away from each other.

That makes the train float above the rails. It's a fast way to travel!

train

rail

magnets

YOUR TURN!

The maglev train can go so fast because it floats just a little bit above its tracks, thanks to magnets. Can you make magnets pull and push on each other? Try it and see!

What You'll Need:

Two bar magnets

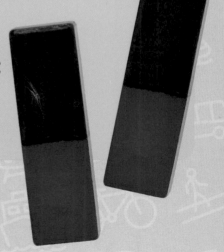

1. Put one magnet flat on the table.
2. Put the other magnet flat on the table so that the ends of the magnets are pointing right at each other. Leave a little bit of space between the magnets.
3. Slowly slide one magnet toward the other magnet. What happens?

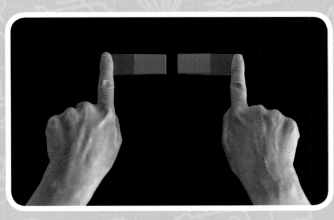

4. Turn one of the magnets around so the other end is facing the other magnet. What happens this time?

Magnets can either attract (pull on) or repel (push on) each other. If the magnets moved toward each other, they pulled on each other. If they moved apart, then they pushed on each other. Maglev trains use both the pulling and pushing power of magnets to make the trains move at super speeds!

CHAPTER 4

People Power!

Some ways to travel need people to make them move! It can be **difficult** to move a handcar. The riders have to push up and down to make the car go.

 Riding on one wheel looks **difficult**. But people learn to do it!

YOU
READ

Walking on stilts is fun! These kids are **high** off the ground. Being on stilts helps them see far away.

People use bikes to get around. The seat on this one is very **high**!

Water in this canal freezes in the winter. It makes a **smooth** sheet of ice. People can ice-skate through the city.

Lots of people like to roll. It is easy to rollerblade on the **smooth** street.

These taxis are like bikes!
Many drivers wait in a line.
They are ready to take people
from place to place.

 Many people can ride this bike at once!

Would you cross a river in a pumpkin? Or ride on a raft made of milk cartons? People make boats from all sorts of **different** things!

There are so many **different** ways to get from here to there!

YOUR TURN!

Draw a boat, car, or other way to get from here to there. Then tell a story about your picture. Where is it going? What is it carrying?

For Abby, who knows all of the verbs. —J.S.

The author and publisher gratefully acknowledge the expert literacy review of Kimberly Gillow, principal, Chelsea School District, Michigan.

Illustration Credits
AL=Alamy Stock Photo; GI=Getty Images; SS=Shutterstock
Cover, Photolife/GI; 1, Yaorusheng/GI; 2 UP (throughout), maljuk/SS; 3, Oliver Hitchen/SS; 4-5, Michel Setboun/GI; 6, WS Collection/AL; 7, Marc Dozier/Hemis/AL; 8, Arvind Yadav/Hindustan Times via GI; 9, Giulia Marchi/Bloomberg via GI; 10, Cherry-Merry/SS; 10-11 (BACKGROUND), IhorZigor/SS; 11 (UP), Robert Kneschke/SS; 11 (CTR RT), ltdedigos/SS; 11 (CTR LE), Peter Atkinson/AL; 11 (LO), Sundry Photography/SS; 12-13, Ted Streshinsky/Corbis/Corbis via GI; 14, GI for Ameriquest; 15 (UP), blickwinkel/Krieger/AL; 15 (LO), Jim Lozouski/SS; 16, Samot/SS; 17 (UP), Olga Koberidze/SS; 17 (LO), NiglayNik/SS; 18 (LO), i viewfinder/SS; 18 (UP), vaalaa/SS; 19, Arsgera/GI; 20, Jeff Rotman/GI; 21, Omar Chatriwala/GI; 22 (UP), Westend61/GI; 22 (LO), Vladimirovic/GI; 23, Ilia Baksheev/SS; 24 (UP), Hilary Andrews/NG Staff; 24 (LO), Hilary Andrews/NG Staff; 24-25 (BACKGROUND), IhorZigor/SS; 25 (UP), Hilary Andrews/NG Staff; 25 (CTR LE), Hilary Andrews/NG Staff; 25 (CTR RT), Hilary Andrews/NG Staff; 25 (LO), Hilary Andrews/NG Staff; 26-27, CasPhotography/GI; 27, David Stock/AL; 28, pejft/GI; 29, John Pyle/Icon SMI/Icon Sport Media via GI; 30, Marc Sanchez/Icon Sportswire via GI; 31, Ev. Safronov/SS; 32-33, cyo bo/SS; 33 (INSET), Martin Bond/Science Source; 34, Nutchanon_Shi/SS; 34-35 (BACKGROUND), IhorZigor/SS; 35 (UP), Hilary Andrews/NG Staff; 35 (LO), Hilary Andrews/NG Staff; 36, Mikhail Starodubov/SS; 37, Goddard New Era/AL; 38, Peter Adams/GI; 39, Andrew Matthews - EMPICS/PA Images via GI; 40, Vladone/GI; 41, Tom Stewart/GI; 42 (UP), Paul McKinnon/SS; 42 (LO), RosaIreneBetancourt 7/AL; 43, Alex Ramsay/AL; 44, Silas Stein/AFP/GI; 45, ArtMarie/GI; 46-47 (crayons), Charles Brutlag/Dreamstime; 46-47 (drawing), Kiefer Flynn

Library of Congress Cataloging-in-Publication Data

Names: Szymanski, Jennifer, author. | National Geographic Kids (Firm), publisher.
Title: Here to there / by Jennifer Szymanski.
Description: Washington, DC : National Geographic Kids, [2019] | Series: National Geographic readers | Audience: Ages 4-6. | Audience: K to Grade 3.
Identifiers: LCCN 2018057775 (print)| LCCN 2019000432 (ebook) | ISBN 9781426334979 (e-book) | ISBN 9781426334955 (pbk.) | ISBN 9781426334962 (hardcover)
Subjects: LCSH: Transportation--Juvenile literature. | CYAC: Transportation.
Classification: LCC HE152 (ebook) | LCC HE152 .S99 2019 (print) | DDC 388--dc23
LC record available at https://lccn.loc.gov/2018057775

Printed in the United States of America
19/WOR/1